Color the Words of Florence Scovel Shinn i curated collection of affirmations from the books, Your word is your Wand, The Game of Life and How To Play It, The Secret Door to Success and The Power of the Spoken Word. This coloring book is for everyone who loves to enjoy the relaxing act of coloring whilst affirming these wonderful powerful words and imprinting them onto the subconscious in the most beautiful and influential way. Florence Scovel Shinn was a master at using words with great effect. It is a very powerful process as it is proven that when we relax our minds, which is achieved through the art of coloring, the affirmation will imprint easily and deeply and realize itself into our reality. Each coloring page contains a unique design, some intricate some less so depending on how you feel. The back of each page is darkened to minimize bleed through and disruption of other pages. I recommend coloring pencils for this book. Following each design there is a scripting page, providing the space to write out exactly your perfect desire with complete faith that this is here for you right now. To make this already powerful combination of coloring affirmations and scripting fail proof, there is a affirmation checklist for each day of the week where it is recommended to repeat the phrase 20 times, 3 times per day.

"My endless good now comes to me in endless ways"

I HAVE PERFECT
CONFIDENCE IN
GOD AND GOD
HAS PERFECT
CONFIDENCE
IN ME

Affirmation Checklist

Monday

AM Affirmations ☐

Midday Affirmations ☐

PM Affirmations ☐

Scripting ☐

Tuesday

AM Affirmations ☐

Midday Affirmations ☐

PM Affirmations ☐

Scripting ☐

Wednesday

AM Affirmations ☐

Midday Affirmations ☐

PM Affirmations ☐

Scripting ☐

Thursday

AM Affirmations ☐

Midday Affirmations ☐

PM Affirmations ☐

Scripting ☐

Friday

AM Affirmations ☐

Midday Affirmations ☐

PM Affirmations ☐

Scripting ☐

Saturday

AM Affirmations ☐

Midday Affirmations ☐

PM Affirmations ☐

Scripting ☐

Sunday

AM Affirmations ☐

Midday Affirmations ☐

PM Affirmations ☐

Scripting ☐

ALL ENEMY
THOUGHTS ARE
WIPED OUT.
I AM
VICTORIOUS

Affirmation Checklist

Monday

AM Affirmations ☐

Midday Affirmations ☐

PM Affirmations ☐

Scripting ☐

Tuesday

AM Affirmations ☐

Midday Affirmations ☐

PM Affirmations ☐

Scripting ☐

Wednesday

AM Affirmations ☐

Midday Affirmations ☐

PM Affirmations ☐

Scripting ☐

Thursday

AM Affirmations ☐

Midday Affirmations ☐

PM Affirmations ☐

Scripting ☐

Friday

AM Affirmations ☐

Midday Affirmations ☐

PM Affirmations ☐

Scripting ☐

Saturday

AM Affirmations ☐

Midday Affirmations ☐

PM Affirmations ☐

Scripting ☐

Sunday

AM Affirmations ☐

Midday Affirmations ☐

PM Affirmations ☐

Scripting ☐

I GIVE THANKS
FOR MY
WHIRLWIND
SUCCESS

Affirmation Checklist

Monday

AM Affirmations

Midday Affirmations

PM Affirmations

Scripting

Tuesday

AM Affirmations

Midday Affirmations

PM Affirmations

Scripting

Wednesday

AM Affirmations

Midday Affirmations

PM Affirmations

Scripting

Thursday

AM Affirmations

Midday Affirmations

PM Affirmations

Scripting

Friday

AM Affirmations

Midday Affirmations

PM Affirmations

Scripting

Saturday

AM Affirmations

Midday Affirmations

PM Affirmations

Scripting

Sunday

AM Affirmations

Midday Affirmations

PM Affirmations

Scripting

GOD'S PROMISES ARE BUILT UPON A ROCK. AS I HAVE ASKED I MUST RECEIVE.

GOD'S PROMISES
ARE BUILT UPON A
ROCK.
AS I HAVE ASKED
I MUST RECEIVE

Affirmation Checklist

Monday

AM Affirmations ☐

Midday Affirmations ☐

PM Affirmations ☐

Scripting ☐

Tuesday

AM Affirmations ☐

Midday Affirmations ☐

PM Affirmations ☐

Scripting ☐

Wednesday

AM Affirmations ☐

Midday Affirmations ☐

PM Affirmations ☐

Scripting ☐

Thursday

AM Affirmations ☐

Midday Affirmations ☐

PM Affirmations ☐

Scripting ☐

Friday

AM Affirmations ☐

Midday Affirmations ☐

PM Affirmations ☐

Scripting ☐

Saturday

AM Affirmations ☐

Midday Affirmations ☐

PM Affirmations ☐

Scripting ☐

Sunday

AM Affirmations ☐

Midday Affirmations ☐

PM Affirmations ☐

Scripting ☐

AS I AM ONE WITH GOD I AM NOW ONE WITH MY HEART'S DESIRE.

AS I AM ONE WITH
GOD
I AM NOW ONE
WITH MY
HEART'S DESIRE

Affirmation Checklist

Monday

AM Affirmations ☐

Midday Affirmations ☐

PM Affirmations ☐

Scripting ☐

Tuesday

AM Affirmations ☐

Midday Affirmations ☐

PM Affirmations ☐

Scripting ☐

Wednesday

AM Affirmations ☐

Midday Affirmations ☐

PM Affirmations ☐

Scripting ☐

Thursday

AM Affirmations ☐

Midday Affirmations ☐

PM Affirmations ☐

Scripting ☐

Friday

AM Affirmations ☐

Midday Affirmations ☐

PM Affirmations ☐

Scripting ☐

Saturday

AM Affirmations ☐

Midday Affirmations ☐

PM Affirmations ☐

Scripting ☐

Sunday

AM Affirmations ☐

Midday Affirmations ☐

PM Affirmations ☐

Scripting ☐

THE WARRIOR
WITHIN ME
AS ALREADY
WON

Affirmation Checklist

Monday

AM Affirmations ☐

Midday Affirmations ☐

PM Affirmations ☐

Scripting ☐

Tuesday

AM Affirmations ☐

Midday Affirmations ☐

PM Affirmations ☐

Scripting ☐

Wednesday

AM Affirmations ☐

Midday Affirmations ☐

PM Affirmations ☐

Scripting ☐

Thursday

AM Affirmations ☐

Midday Affirmations ☐

PM Affirmations ☐

Scripting ☐

Friday

AM Affirmations ☐

Midday Affirmations ☐

PM Affirmations ☐

Scripting ☐

Saturday

AM Affirmations ☐

Midday Affirmations ☐

PM Affirmations ☐

Scripting ☐

Sunday

AM Affirmations ☐

Midday Affirmations ☐

PM Affirmations ☐

Scripting ☐

MY GOOD NOW FLOWS
TO ME IN A STEADY
UNBROKEN, EVER-INCREASING

STREAM OF SUCCESS,
HAPPINESS
AND ABUNDANCE

MY GOOD NOW
FLOWS TO ME
IN A STEADY
UNBROKEN,
EVER-INCREASING
STREAM OF SUCCESS,
HAPPINESS
AND ABUNDANCE.

Affirmation Checklist

Monday

AM Affirmations ☐

Midday Affirmations ☐

PM Affirmations ☐

Scripting ☐

Tuesday

AM Affirmations ☐

Midday Affirmations ☐

PM Affirmations ☐

Scripting ☐

Wednesday

AM Affirmations ☐

Midday Affirmations ☐

PM Affirmations ☐

Scripting ☐

Thursday

AM Affirmations ☐

Midday Affirmations ☐

PM Affirmations ☐

Scripting ☐

Friday

AM Affirmations ☐

Midday Affirmations ☐

PM Affirmations ☐

Scripting ☐

Saturday

AM Affirmations ☐

Midday Affirmations ☐

PM Affirmations ☐

Scripting ☐

Sunday

AM Affirmations ☐

Midday Affirmations ☐

PM Affirmations ☐

Scripting ☐

ALL LACK,
LIMITATION AND
FAILURE ARE WIPED
OUT OF MY
CONSCIOUSNESS

Affirmation Checklist

Monday

AM Affirmations ☐

Midday Affirmations ☐

PM Affirmations ☐

Scripting ☐

Tuesday

AM Affirmations ☐

Midday Affirmations ☐

PM Affirmations ☐

Scripting ☐

Wednesday

AM Affirmations ☐

Midday Affirmations ☐

PM Affirmations ☐

Scripting ☐

Thursday

AM Affirmations ☐

Midday Affirmations ☐

PM Affirmations ☐

Scripting ☐

Friday

AM Affirmations ☐

Midday Affirmations ☐

PM Affirmations ☐

Scripting ☐

Saturday

AM Affirmations ☐

Midday Affirmations ☐

PM Affirmations ☐

Scripting ☐

Sunday

AM Affirmations ☐

Midday Affirmations ☐

PM Affirmations ☐

Scripting ☐

GOD IS MY
UNFAILING AND
IMMEDIATE
SUPPLY OF ALL GOOD

Affirmation Checklist

Monday

AM Affirmations	☐
Midday Affirmations	☐
PM Affirmations	☐
Scripting	☐

Tuesday

AM Affirmations	☐
Midday Affirmations	☐
PM Affirmations	☐
Scripting	☐

Wednesday

AM Affirmations	☐
Midday Affirmations	☐
PM Affirmations	☐
Scripting	☐

Thursday

AM Affirmations	☐
Midday Affirmations	☐
PM Affirmations	☐
Scripting	☐

Friday

AM Affirmations	☐
Midday Affirmations	☐
PM Affirmations	☐
Scripting	☐

Saturday

AM Affirmations	☐
Midday Affirmations	☐
PM Affirmations	☐
Scripting	☐

Sunday

AM Affirmations	☐
Midday Affirmations	☐
PM Affirmations	☐
Scripting	☐

MY ANGEL OF
DESTINY
GOES BEFORE ME,
KEEPING ME IN THE
WAY

Affirmation Checklist

Monday

AM Affirmations ☐

Midday Affirmations ☐

PM Affirmations ☐

Scripting ☐

Tuesday

AM Affirmations ☐

Midday Affirmations ☐

PM Affirmations ☐

Scripting ☐

Wednesday

AM Affirmations ☐

Midday Affirmations ☐

PM Affirmations ☐

Scripting ☐

Thursday

AM Affirmations ☐

Midday Affirmations ☐

PM Affirmations ☐

Scripting ☐

Friday

AM Affirmations ☐

Midday Affirmations ☐

PM Affirmations ☐

Scripting ☐

Saturday

AM Affirmations ☐

Midday Affirmations ☐

PM Affirmations ☐

Scripting ☐

Sunday

AM Affirmations ☐

Midday Affirmations ☐

PM Affirmations ☐

Scripting ☐

my happiness is
gods affair,
therefore, no
one can interfere

MY HAPPINESS IS
GOD'S AFFAIR,
THEREFORE,
NO ONE CAN
INTERFERE

Affirmation Checklist

Monday

AM Affirmations ☐

Midday Affirmations ☐

PM Affirmations ☐

Scripting ☐

Tuesday

AM Affirmations ☐

Midday Affirmations ☐

PM Affirmations ☐

Scripting ☐

Wednesday

AM Affirmations ☐

Midday Affirmations ☐

PM Affirmations ☐

Scripting ☐

Thursday

AM Affirmations ☐

Midday Affirmations ☐

PM Affirmations ☐

Scripting ☐

Friday

AM Affirmations ☐

Midday Affirmations ☐

PM Affirmations ☐

Scripting ☐

Saturday

AM Affirmations ☐

Midday Affirmations ☐

PM Affirmations ☐

Scripting ☐

Sunday

AM Affirmations ☐

Midday Affirmations ☐

PM Affirmations ☐

Scripting ☐

LET ME NEVER WANDER

FROM MY HEART'S DESIRE

LET ME NEVER
WANDER FROM MY
HEART'S DESIRE

Affirmation Checklist

Monday

AM Affirmations ☐

Midday Affirmations ☐

PM Affirmations ☐

Scripting ☐

Tuesday

AM Affirmations ☐

Midday Affirmations ☐

PM Affirmations ☐

Scripting ☐

Wednesday

AM Affirmations ☐

Midday Affirmations ☐

PM Affirmations ☐

Scripting ☐

Thursday

AM Affirmations ☐

Midday Affirmations ☐

PM Affirmations ☐

Scripting ☐

Friday

AM Affirmations ☐

Midday Affirmations ☐

PM Affirmations ☐

Scripting ☐

Saturday

AM Affirmations ☐

Midday Affirmations ☐

PM Affirmations ☐

Scripting ☐

Sunday

AM Affirmations ☐

Midday Affirmations ☐

PM Affirmations ☐

Scripting ☐

I AM HARMONIOUS, POISED, AND MAGNETIC. I NOW DRAW TO MYSELF MY OWN.

I AM HARMONIOUS,
POISED AND MAGNETIC,
I NOW DRAW TO
MYSELF MY OWN

Affirmation Checklist

Monday

AM Affirmations ☐

Midday Affirmations ☐

PM Affirmations ☐

Scripting ☐

Tuesday

AM Affirmations ☐

Midday Affirmations ☐

PM Affirmations ☐

Scripting ☐

Wednesday

AM Affirmations ☐

Midday Affirmations ☐

PM Affirmations ☐

Scripting ☐

Thursday

AM Affirmations ☐

Midday Affirmations ☐

PM Affirmations ☐

Scripting ☐

Friday

AM Affirmations ☐

Midday Affirmations ☐

PM Affirmations ☐

Scripting ☐

Saturday

AM Affirmations ☐

Midday Affirmations ☐

PM Affirmations ☐

Scripting ☐

Sunday

AM Affirmations ☐

Midday Affirmations ☐

PM Affirmations ☐

Scripting ☐

Your Word Is Your Wand Scripting Page

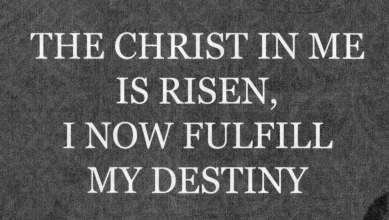

THE CHRIST IN ME
IS RISEN,
I NOW FULFILL
MY DESTINY

Affirmation Checklist

Monday

AM Affirmations ☐

Midday Affirmations ☐

PM Affirmations ☐

Scripting ☐

Tuesday

AM Affirmations ☐

Midday Affirmations ☐

PM Affirmations ☐

Scripting ☐

Wednesday

AM Affirmations ☐

Midday Affirmations ☐

PM Affirmations ☐

Scripting ☐

Thursday

AM Affirmations ☐

Midday Affirmations ☐

PM Affirmations ☐

Scripting ☐

Friday

AM Affirmations ☐

Midday Affirmations ☐

PM Affirmations ☐

Scripting ☐

Saturday

AM Affirmations ☐

Midday Affirmations ☐

PM Affirmations ☐

Scripting ☐

Sunday

AM Affirmations ☐

Midday Affirmations ☐

PM Affirmations ☐

Scripting ☐

DIVINE IDEAS NEVER CONFLICT

DIVINE IDEAS
NEVER CONFLICT

Affirmation Checklist

Monday

AM Affirmations ☐

Midday Affirmations ☐

PM Affirmations ☐

Scripting ☐

Tuesday

AM Affirmations ☐

Midday Affirmations ☐

PM Affirmations ☐

Scripting ☐

Wednesday

AM Affirmations ☐

Midday Affirmations ☐

PM Affirmations ☐

Scripting ☐

Thursday

AM Affirmations ☐

Midday Affirmations ☐

PM Affirmations ☐

Scripting ☐

Friday

AM Affirmations ☐

Midday Affirmations ☐

PM Affirmations ☐

Scripting ☐

Saturday

AM Affirmations ☐

Midday Affirmations ☐

PM Affirmations ☐

Scripting ☐

Sunday

AM Affirmations ☐

Midday Affirmations ☐

PM Affirmations ☐

Scripting ☐

MY ENDLESS GOOD
NOW COMES TO ME
IN ENDLESS WAYS

Affirmation Checklist

Monday

AM Affirmations ☐

Midday Affirmations ☐

PM Affirmations ☐

Scripting ☐

Tuesday

AM Affirmations ☐

Midday Affirmations ☐

PM Affirmations ☐

Scripting ☐

Wednesday

AM Affirmations ☐

Midday Affirmations ☐

PM Affirmations ☐

Scripting ☐

Thursday

AM Affirmations ☐

Midday Affirmations ☐

PM Affirmations ☐

Scripting ☐

Friday

AM Affirmations ☐

Midday Affirmations ☐

PM Affirmations ☐

Scripting ☐

Saturday

AM Affirmations ☐

Midday Affirmations ☐

PM Affirmations ☐

Scripting ☐

Sunday

AM Affirmations ☐

Midday Affirmations ☐

PM Affirmations ☐

Scripting ☐

I HAVE A WONDERFUL JOY IN A WONDERFUL WAY, AND MY WONDERFUL JOY HAS COME TO STAY.

I HAVE
WONDERFUL
JOY IN A
WONDERFUL
WAY AND MY
WONDERFUL JOY
HAS COME TO STAY

Affirmation Checklist

Monday

AM Affirmations ☐

Midday Affirmations ☐

PM Affirmations ☐

Scripting ☐

Tuesday

AM Affirmations ☐

Midday Affirmations ☐

PM Affirmations ☐

Scripting ☐

Wednesday

AM Affirmations ☐

Midday Affirmations ☐

PM Affirmations ☐

Scripting ☐

Thursday

AM Affirmations ☐

Midday Affirmations ☐

PM Affirmations ☐

Scripting ☐

Friday

AM Affirmations ☐

Midday Affirmations ☐

PM Affirmations ☐

Scripting ☐

Saturday

AM Affirmations ☐

Midday Affirmations ☐

PM Affirmations ☐

Scripting ☐

Sunday

AM Affirmations ☐

Midday Affirmations ☐

PM Affirmations ☐

Scripting ☐

I NOW JUMP
INTO MY GOOD

Affirmation Checklist

Monday

AM Affirmations ☐

Midday Affirmations ☐

PM Affirmations ☐

Scripting ☐

Tuesday

AM Affirmations ☐

Midday Affirmations ☐

PM Affirmations ☐

Scripting ☐

Wednesday

AM Affirmations ☐

Midday Affirmations ☐

PM Affirmations ☐

Scripting ☐

Thursday

AM Affirmations ☐

Midday Affirmations ☐

PM Affirmations ☐

Scripting ☐

Friday

AM Affirmations ☐

Midday Affirmations ☐

PM Affirmations ☐

Scripting ☐

Saturday

AM Affirmations ☐

Midday Affirmations ☐

PM Affirmations ☐

Scripting ☐

Sunday

AM Affirmations ☐

Midday Affirmations ☐

PM Affirmations ☐

Scripting ☐

I CAST EVERY BURDEN ON THE CHRIST WITHIN AND I GO FREE!

I CAST EVERY
BURDEN ON THE
CHRIST WITHIN
AND I GO FREE

Affirmation Checklist

Monday

AM Affirmations	☐
Midday Affirmations	☐
PM Affirmations	☐
Scripting	☐

Tuesday

AM Affirmations	☐
Midday Affirmations	☐
PM Affirmations	☐
Scripting	☐

Wednesday

AM Affirmations	☐
Midday Affirmations	☐
PM Affirmations	☐
Scripting	☐

Thursday

AM Affirmations	☐
Midday Affirmations	☐
PM Affirmations	☐
Scripting	☐

Friday

AM Affirmations	☐
Midday Affirmations	☐
PM Affirmations	☐
Scripting	☐

Saturday

AM Affirmations	☐
Midday Affirmations	☐
PM Affirmations	☐
Scripting	☐

Sunday

AM Affirmations	☐
Midday Affirmations	☐
PM Affirmations	☐
Scripting	☐

Printed in Great Britain
by Amazon